Kids Talk About

Sharing

by Carrie Finn

illustrated by Amy Bailey Muehlenhardt

Donation Box

PICTURE WINDOW BOOKS
Minneapolis, Minnesota

Special thanks to our advisers for their expertise:

Dr. Kay Herting Wahl, Director of School Counseling
University of Minnesota

Susan Kesselring, M.A., Literacy Educator
Rosemount–Apple Valley–Eagan (Minnesota) School District

Editor: Christianne Jones

Designer: Joe Anderson

Page Production: Brandie Shoemaker

Editorial Director: Carol Jones

Creative Director: Keith Griffin

The illustrations in this book were created digitally.

Picture Window Books

151 Good Counsel Drive

P.O. Box 669

Mankato, MN 56002-0669

877-845-8392

www.picturewindowbooks.com

Printed in the United States of America.

All books published by Picture Window Books
are manufactured using paper containing at least
10 percent post-consumer waste.

Photo Credit: Benno Friedman/Time Life, page 30

Library of Congress Cataloging-in-Publication Data

Finn, Carrie.

Kids talk about sharing / by Carrie Finn ; illustrated by Amy Bailey Muehlenhardt.

p. cm. – (Kids talk junior)

Includes bibliographical references and index.

ISBN-13: 978-1-4048-2319-8 (hardcover)

ISBN-10: 1-4048-2319-0 (hardcover)

1. Sharing—Juvenile literature. I. Muehlenhardt, Amy Bailey, 1974- ill. II. Title. III. Series.

BJ1533.G4F56 2007

177'.7–dc22

2006003403

Kids Talk Jr.

COUNSELOR: Kendra

Hi, Friends!

My name is Kendra Kemp. I'm in the fifth grade at Newton Elementary School. My friends call me "Kind Kendra." My favorite thing to do is to give advice and help others.

Lately I have been reading a bunch of letters about sharing. Sharing is hard to do sometimes. Read on to learn what I have to say about sharing.

Sincerely,

Kendra

Dear Kendra,

My grandma gave me money for my birthday. I bought a big bag of candy with it. My mom says I have to share with my little sister. Do I have to?

JoAnn

Kids Talk Jr.

COUNSELOR: Kendra

Dear JoAnn,

Sharing can be hard, especially when you have to share something you really like. Would you like your sister to share with you? If you said yes, then you should share with her.

Kendra

Dear Kendra,

In school we are working on a big group project. I'm afraid all of the kids will laugh at my ideas. What should I do?

Callie

Kids Talk Jr.

COUNSELOR: Kendra

Dear Callie,

Don't be afraid to share your ideas. Some of the best projects get done because people share their ideas.

Kendra

Dear Kendra,

On the news they were talking about people who don't have enough money to buy winter clothes. How can I help?

Delia

Kids Talk Jr.

COUNSELOR: Kendra

Dear Delia,

Talk to your parents and your teacher about starting a sharing tree. Have kids in your class bring mittens, coats, or scarves to share. A teacher or parent can help you make sure the clothes get to the people who need them.

Kendra

Dear Kendra,

I have to share my bedroom with my cousin when she comes to visit. Why can't she sleep on the couch?

Tammy

Kids Talk Jr.

COUNSELOR: Kendra

Dear Tammy,

Your cousin probably likes sleeping in your room. It makes her feel safe while she's away from home. Just think of it as a slumber party. Have fun!

Kendra

Dear Kendra,

I'd like to teach my friend Mike how to skateboard. Do you think that's a good idea?

Kirby

COUNSELOR: Kendra

Dear Kirby,

Sharing your talents with others is a great idea! I'm sure that Mike will appreciate it. Ask Mike if he has a talent he would like to share with you.

Kendra

Dear Kendra,

I really like playing games on the computer. But my brother is always using it. How can I make him share?

Joel

Kids Talk Jr.

COUNSELOR: Kendra

Dear Joel,

Ask your mom or dad to set a time limit for each of you. Then you both get equal time for your games. Better yet, find a game that you can play together.

Kendra

Dear Kendra,

My dad wants me to help him rake the yard. It's such
a big yard. How can we get it all done?

Luke

Kids Talk Jr.

COUNSELOR: Kendra

Dear Luke,

You and your dad should decide which parts of the lawn each of you
is going to rake. Once you divide up the job, it won't seem like such
a huge project.

Kendra

Dear Kendra,

My mom told me that I have to give away all of my old toys. Why should I give my cool stuff to people I don't even know?

Pamela

Kids Talk Jr.

COUNSELOR: Kendra

Dear Pamela,

This kind of sharing is called charity. Charity means that you give things to people who really need them. If you aren't using your toys anymore, the best thing to do is to share them with someone who will.

Kendra

Dear Kendra,

When my friends and I were playing soccer, we broke a window. I got caught and have to pay for the window. Shouldn't my friends have to pay, too?

Benjamin

Kids Talk Jr.

COUNSELOR: Kendra

Dear Benjamin,

Sometimes part of sharing is sharing the consequences of your actions. Tell your friends that they are also responsible for the accident. With a nice reminder, they will probably be willing to share in the cost.

Kendra

Dear Kendra,

I heard a funny story about a girl in my class. I want to tell all my friends. My brother says I shouldn't repeat the story. Why not?

Jordan

Kids Talk Jr.

COUNSELOR: Kendra

Dear Jordan,

Your brother is right. You aren't sharing a story, you are gossiping. A story that makes someone feel bad is not the kind of story you should be sharing.

Kendra

Kids Talk Jr.

COUNSELOR: Kendra

That's all the time I have for today. I have to get to my dance class. I hope I answered all of your questions about sharing. There's plenty more to read about. Turn the page to learn more about sharing!

Sincerely,

Kendra

Grab a piece of paper and a pencil, and take this fun quiz. Good luck!

1. If your mom tells you to share your candy, you should

   a) only do it if the candy is yucky.

   b) always share because sharing is nice.

   c) never do it because there won't be enough candy for you.

2. It's important to share your ideas with others

   a) because it will help everyone.

   b) as long as your ideas involve pink monkeys.

   c) while jumping on one foot and singing.

3. If you want to start a sharing tree at school, you should talk to

   a) your teacher, your parents, and other kids.

   b) the mayor of your town.

   c) your favorite TV character.

4. Sharing your bedroom with your cousin is good because

   a) your cousin will bring toys with her.

   b) you can help her feel safe.

   c) she will snore really loudly all night.

5. If you teach someone to skateboard, you are sharing your

   a) broccoli.

   b) germs.

   c) talent.

6. If your brother is using the computer when you want to use it, it's a good idea to

    a) have your mom or dad set a time limit so you can share the computer.

    b) sit on the keyboard until he gets off.

    c) play a trumpet right behind him.

7. Raking the lawn is easy if you

    a) pick up each leaf one by one.

    b) share the job with someone else.

    c) wash the leaves with orange juice.

8. Charity is

    a) when you give away the things that you don't use anymore to people
       who need them.

    b) when you keep everything in your closet and don't let anyone else use it.

    c) when you throw your toys in the garbage.

9. Sharing the blame when you break a window means that you are being

    a) a troublemaker.

    b) responsible.

    c) really silly.

10. Gossiping is

    a) a type of vegetable.

    b) when you tell stories about someone else that might not be true.

    c) a game you play in gym.

Jim Henson

Jim Henson started working with puppets when he was in high school. He shared his creativity to bring joy and laughter to people all over the world.

In 1966, Jim Henson and his muppets, as he called them, were put on a new show called "Sesame Street." There he worked with actors and other talented people to create muppets like Ernie and Bert, Grover, Oscar the Grouch, Cookie Monster, and Big Bird. Jim Henson is best known for his creation of the muppet Kermit the Frog.

Even though Jim Henson died in 1990, he will always be remembered as a great artist who shared his muppets with kids everywhere.

Glossary

advice—opinions about what should or should not be done about a problem

appreciate—to value someone or something

charity—when you help someone in need

consequence—the result of an action

gossip—stories that are told about someone behind his or her back

share—to give part of what you have to someone else

talents—special abilities or gifts

To Learn More

AT THE LIBRARY

Amos, Janine. *Sharing*. Milwaukee: Gareth Stevens Pub., 2002.

Kyle, Kathryn. *Sharing*. Chanhassen, Minn.: Child's World, 2003.

Meiners, Cheri J. *Share and Take Turns*. Minneapolis: Free Spirit Pub., 2003.

ON THE WEB

FactHound offers a safe, fun way to find Internet sites related to this book.

All of the sites on FactHound have been researched by our staff.

1. Visit *www.facthound.com*

2. Type in this special code

   for age-appropriate sites: 1404823190

3. Click on the FETCH IT button.

Your trusty FactHound will fetch the best sites for you!

Index

Look for all of the books in the Kids Talk Jr. series:

Kids Talk About Bravery	1-4048-2314-X
Kids Talk About Bullying	1-4048-2315-8
Kids Talk About Fairness	1-4048-2316-6
Kids Talk About Honesty	1-4048-2317-4
Kids Talk About Respect	1-4048-2318-2
Kids Talk About Sharing	1-4048-2319-0